STECK-VAUGHN
ACHIEVE
New York State
English/Language Arts
6

Harcourt Achieve
Rigby · Saxon · Steck-Vaughn

www.HarcourtAchieve.com
1.800.531.5015

ACKNOWLEDGMENTS

©CORBIS, p. 29, Steck Vaughn Collection

The New York State Testing Program in English Language Arts is published by CTB/McGraw-Hill. Such company has neither endorsed nor authorized this test-preparation book.

ISBN 1-4190-0939-7

© 2006 Harcourt Achieve Inc.

All rights reserved. No part of the material protected by this copyright may be reproduced or utilized in any form or by any means, in whole or in part, without permission in writing from the copyright owner. Requests for permission should be mailed to: Copyright Permissions, Harcourt Achieve, P.O. Box 27010, Austin, TX 78755.

Rigby and Steck-Vaughn are trademarks of Harcourt Achieve Inc. registered in the United States of America and/or other jurisdictions.

5 6 7 8 9 10 862 11 10 09

Achieve New York State Contents

New York State English Language Arts Standards.......... 2
To the Student: About Achieve New York State............ 3

NYS Testing Program Modeled Instruction
    Reading 1... 4
    Reading 2... 12
    Listening 18
Test-Taking Tips... 22

Practice Test for New York State English Language Arts
    Book 1 23
        Session 1 25
    Book 2 41
        Session 2 43
        Session 3 51
NYS Testing Program Answer Sheet..................... 61

New York State English Language Arts Standards

Standard 1: **Students will read for information and understanding.**
Students will write for information and understanding.
Students will listen for information and understanding.

- Use text to understand vocabulary
- Draw conclusions
- Understand stated information
- Make basic inferences
- Recognize and use organizational features
- Locate information in a text
- Identify main idea
- Identify supporting details
- Compare and contrast information

Standard 2: **Students will read for literary response and expression.**
Students will write for literary response and expression.
Students will listen for literary response and expression.

- Use figurative language to interpret text
- Make inferences about story events or characters
- Use key vocabulary to interpret text
- Describe characters and their motivations
- Understand features that distinguish genres
- Recognize how author's language use creates feelings
- Interpret plot
- Draw conclusions
- Interpret theme

Standard 3: **Students will read for critical analysis and evaluation.**
Students will write for critical analysis and evaluation.
Students will listen for critical analysis and evaluation.

- Distinguish between fact and opinion
- Use critical analysis to evaluate information
- Use critical analysis to evaluate ideas
- Identify author's purpose

To the Student: About Achieve New York State

This book will help you prepare for the New York State English Language Arts Test. The first part of the book lets you practice on different kinds of questions you will see on the real test. It also gives you tips for answering each question.

The second part of the book is a practice test that is similar to the New York State English Language Arts Test. Taking this test will help you know what the actual test is like.

The New York State English Language Arts Test includes questions about reading, listening, and writing. It will ask you to write about what you have listened to and read. Test questions will help measure how well you understand the skills outlined in the New York State Learning Standards.

Kinds of Questions

Multiple-choice Questions

After each multiple-choice question are four answer choices. For the Modeled Instruction part of this book, you will circle the letter next to the correct answer. For the Practice Test, use the separate Answer Sheet and fill in the circle that has the same letter as your answer. Remember to pick the choice that you think is the best answer.

Open-ended Questions

These questions will not give you answer choices. You will need to write out your answers. There are two kinds of open-ended questions:

- **Short-response Questions**

  These questions will be scored on reading or listening comprehension. They will not be scored on writing.

- **Extended-response Questions**

  This question has its own symbol. When you see this symbol next to a question, you know this question will be scored on reading or listening comprehension and on writing. Be sure to plan before you write and check your writing for correct grammar, punctuation, capitalization, spelling, and paragraph organization.

NYS Modeled Instruction: Reading 1

DIRECTIONS: In this section, you are going to read two passages. Then you will answer questions about what you have read. Circle the letter of the correct answer.

The following article tells about the Iroquois people. Read "Kainerekowa." Then do Numbers 1 through 8.

Kainerekowa

For hundreds of years, the Iroquois people filled the land between the Adirondack Mountains and Niagara Falls. Their population grew and they became strong. Some Iroquois, though, fought each other, often to the death. The Iroquois were in danger of dying out.

Then a man showed up whose name was *Deganawida*. Deganawida means "Two River Currents Flowing Together." He wanted peace. He told the Iroquois they must live in harmony with each other. At first, the Iroquois did not listen. But in 1451, Deganawida gave a speech on the day of a solar eclipse. Most Iroquois did not know what eclipses were, but they seemed to be a sign to listen. They believed that Deganawida had used special powers to block out the sun. They eagerly listened to his message.

confederacy = a group of people who join together for a common purpose

This is how the Iroquois Confederacy was created. The members of the new group agreed to follow *Kainerekowa*, the Great Law of Peace. The most essential part of the law was that the Iroquois could no longer kill each other. Also, the confederacy made decisions on all important issues about the tribe.

The confederacy was led by fifty peace chiefs, called *sachems*. Sachems often wore head dresses made of deer antlers. They were elected by the tribal mothers. Sachems came from several different tribes, including the Onandaga, Cayuga, Oneida, Mohawk, and Seneca. The Tuscarora tribe joined in 1722. Sachems were the decision makers for the confederacy.

Thanks to the Iroquois Confederacy, the Iroquois soon grew united and powerful. Some tribes were adopted into Iroquois culture. They drove other native tribes out of the area so that they could expand their territory.

By 1660, Europeans began to enter the New World. Settlers from France, Britain, and Spain all arrived. The sachems of the Iroquois Confederacy met with the Europeans to establish peaceful relations. Soon, the Iroquois were trading with the settlers, and sometimes they sold land to the Europeans. But as more and more Europeans showed up, things got worse for the Iroquois. The arrival of so many new people diminished the number of Iroquois people. This was mainly because of conflicts with settlers and diseases brought by Europeans. There had been 25,000 Iroquois in 1668. By one hundred years later, fewer than half remained.

| heritage = customs |

The Iroquois people recovered slowly over the next two centuries. In recent years, however, there has been a surge of interest in native pride. This has caused many people to recognize their Iroquois heritage.

| diplomacy = making peace |

Today, there are over 70,000 Iroquois in the United States and Canada, living in peace with each other. The Iroquois still honor Kainerekowa, the Great Law of Peace. Now, members of the Iriquois tribe travel the world to speak about diplomacy. In this way, they are able to share the Kainerekowa with everyone.

Go On

1 Read this sentence from the article:

The most essential part of the law was that the Iroquois could no longer kill each other.

In this sentence, what does *essential* mean?

A ancient

B unusual

C exciting

D important

> **Tip:** To figure out what a word means, decide which meaning would make the most sense in the sentence. Try replacing the word *essential* with each of the four answer choices. Decide which of the choices best fits the meaning of the sentence.

2 Kainerekowa is a name for

F a man

G a peace chief

H a native tribe

J an Iroquois law

> **Tip:** Sometimes the details you need are stated right in the text. Search the article for the word *Kainerekowa* to find out what it means.

3 Which of the following did the Iroquois not do with European settlers?

A sell them land

B try to make peace with them

C drive them away from their land

D trade with them

> **Tip:** You should be able to find evidence in the article to support details. Find the detail that is not supported in the article.

4 According to the beginning of the article, why was the Iroquois tribe in danger of dying out?

F They fought each other.

G They had no land to live on.

H They were killed by settlers.

J They were defeated by other tribes.

> **Tip:** Read the article carefully to recall important details. The question asks you about the beginning of the article. Reread the first paragraph to find out why the Iroquois tribe was in danger of dying out.

New York State English Language Arts Standards
1. (1) Read for information and understanding. Use text to understand vocabulary.
2. (1) Read for information and understanding. Understand stated information.
3. (1) Read for information and understanding. Locate information in a text.
4. (1) Read for information and understanding. Understand stated information.

5 How did sachems come into power?

  A They put themselves in charge.
  B They were picked by Deganawida.
  C They were elected by tribal mothers.
  D They were chosen by the entire tribe.

> **Tip:** Authors include facts in their articles to support ideas. Scan the article and find where it tells about sachems. Reread carefully to figure out how sachems came into power.

6 The Iroquois listened to Deganawida's speech because

  F they realized that their tribe was dying out
  G they believed he used powers to block out the sun
  H he was an important leader of the Iroquois
  J the Iroquois Confederacy told them they should listen

> **Tip:** Sometimes one event in a story causes another event to happen. Look closely at the article. Figure out which event caused the Iroquois to listen to Deganawida's speech.

7 Read this sentence from the article:

The arrival of so many new people diminished the Iroquois population.

In this sentence, what does *diminished* mean?

  A completed
  B destroyed
  C made sad
  D made smaller

> **Tip:** Sometimes you can find out what a word means by looking at the words and phrases around it. Reread the sentence and look for clues that will help you find the meaning of the word *diminished*.

8 Which of these events happened last?

  F The Iroquois agreed to follow Kainerekowa.
  G The Iroquois population was reduced by more than half.
  H Deganawida gave a speech during a solar eclipse.
  J The Tuscarora tribe joined the Iroquois Confederacy.

> **Tip:** Important events in articles are usually given in chronological order. Go back through the article and compare the order in which each of these events happened.

Go On

New York State English Language Arts Standards
5. (1) **Read for information and understanding.** Understand stated information.
6. (1) **Read for information and understanding.** Make basic inferences.
7. (1) **Read for information and understanding.** Use text to understand vocabulary.
8. (1) **Read for information and understanding.** Recognize and use organizational features.

DIRECTIONS: The following article describes whales, which are among the largest animals in the world. Read "Whales." Then do Numbers 9 through 16.

Whales

Just think about it—the largest animal ever known. It could make even the largest dinosaur look small. It's the blue whale! In fact, the blue whale can grow to over ninety-five feet long. This is about the length of two large locomotives!

Whales live in the sea but are not fish. They are mammals. This means that they are warm-blooded and breathe air, just like you. They must hold their breath when they go underwater and would die if they could not come to the surface of the water to breathe air.

Whales, along with dolphins and porpoises, are members of a group of animals called *cetaceans* (suh TAY shunz). There are at least seventy-five different kinds of whales, ranging in size from under ten feet to more than ninety-five feet. Whales are divided into two main groups: toothed whales and baleen whales. A killer whale is a kind of toothed whale. Humpback whales, the huge blue whale, and gray whales are examples of baleen whales.

Whales have a weak sense of smell. They also have poor eyesight deep in the ocean. So, what do they do to find food and their way around? Toothed whales use echolocation, a way of locating something by listening to an echo. These whales make sounds. The sound waves travel underwater. The whales wait to see how long before that sound hits something and sends back an echo. This way, they know how far away an object is from them. Since baleen whales eat differently from toothed whales, they don't seem to use echolocation.

Although most whales swallow their food whole, the toothed whales can hold and bite fish and other sea animals. Baleen whales, on the other hand, have long pieces of bone, or baleen, that hang down from the upper jaw like curtains and look like a fine-toothed comb. The baleen acts as a strainer. When baleen whales take a huge mouthful of seawater, they trap tiny animals and plants that drift in the sea. The water flows out, and the food stays inside for the whales to swallow.

Toothed whales have a single blowhole, while baleen whales have two. A blowhole is used for breathing, like a nose. Most whales can hold their breath for ten minutes or more. The sperm whale, largest of the toothed whales, can dive deeper than any other whale and can stay underwater longer—for more than an hour. Have you ever seen your breath on a cold day? This is similar to what happens when a whale comes to the surface and breathes out. Mists from a blowhole can spray twenty-five feet high!

Whales enjoy being with other whales. They usually live in groups called pods. Some whales, such as blue whales, live in small groups. Others, such as humpbacks, may travel in groups of twenty or more. Some whales even help one another. They can hunt food together. Sometimes, if one whale is sick or injured, another will come to its side.

Some whales migrate, or travel long distances, each year. The humpback and gray whales migrate thousands of miles.

Whales are interesting creatures because of the sounds they make. Their low-pitched sounds can be heard for hundreds of miles. Different types of whales make different types of sounds. The blue whale makes the loudest sound, an enormous grunt. Some people think it is much louder than a jet engine. The killer whale, or orca, is considered the most "talkative." Orcas make different kinds of sounds, from clicks to whistles. Humpback whales are famous for their singing. Their beautiful songs may last for several hours. In fact, songs of the humpback whale have been made into best-selling recordings.

People have hunted whales for hundreds of years. Why do people hunt whales? Whales were once prized for their blubber, or fat. Lamps burned oil made from blubber. Later, other items, such as soap, were made from whale oil. Some people ate whale meat. As more and more whales were killed, people grew concerned about saving them, especially since some kinds of whales were in danger of becoming extinct. In the 1980s, many countries agreed to stop hunting whales. However, pollution continues to be a problem for whales. Anything that makes the water poisonous kills the animals and plants that whales need to eat. In addition, whales are sometimes accidentally caught in large fishing nets. Because these wonderful creatures need protection, many people continue to work to save them.

9 The last paragraph tells mainly about

A how blubber was used to make whale oil

B what products were once made from whales

C why whales are no longer hunted

D why fishing nets can be harmful to whales

Tip: Authors include certain information to support an idea. Skim the last paragraph and figure out which idea is supported by the details included in this paragraph.

10 Which of the following books would provide the most information about humpback whales?

F *Animals of the Sea*

G *Sharks and Whales*

H *Whales of the World*

J *Baleen Whales*

Tip: The title usually gives clues about the content of a book. Books with broad, general titles may have less information about a topic than books with very specific titles. Remember that humpback whales are a kind of baleen whale. Then decide which book would be most useful to find the information you need.

11 What was probably the author's purpose in writing this article?

A to persuade readers not to pollute

B to tell how whales can help people

C to provide information about whales

D to amuse readers with funny whale stories

Tip: Authors may write to convince the reader of something, to explain how to do something, to give the reader information, or to entertain. Scan the article to determine which of these the author tries to do.

12 Read this sentence from the article:

As more and more whales were killed, people grew concerned about saving them, especially since some kinds of whales were in danger of becoming extinct.

In this sentence, the word *extinct* means

F easy to find

G lost forever

H humorous

J unpleasant

Tip: If you read a word you don't know, look at the words and phrases in the sentence where the word appears. Reread this sentence and consider why people were concerned.

New York State English Language Arts Standards
9. (1) **Read for information and understanding.** Make basic inferences.
10. (3) **Read for critical analysis and evaluation.** Use critical analysis to evaluate information.
11. (3) **Read for critical analysis and evaluation.** Identify author's purpose.
12. (1) **Read for information and understanding.** Use text to understand vocabulary.

13 Which of the following is not a reason why people hunted whales?

- A for their oil
- B for their teeth
- C for their meat
- D for their blubber

Tip: Read an article carefully to notice important details. Find the part of the article that tells about why people hunt whales. Figure out which of these reasons is not mentioned.

14 How is a toothed whale different from a baleen whale?

- F A toothed whale has teeth but a baleen whale does not.
- G A toothed whale is a mammal but a baleen whale is not.
- H A toothed whale makes sounds but a baleen whale does not.
- J A toothed whale lives in the sea but a baleen whale does not.

Tip: This question asks you to make a comparison. Reread the information in the article about toothed whales and baleen whales. Then decide what the whales do not have in common.

15 What do toothed whales use to find their way around?

- A blowholes
- B sense of smell
- C their bones
- D echolocation

Tip: To find details in an article, skim the article for the words in each answer choice. Choose the answer that explains how toothed whales find their way around.

16 Which sentence from the story expresses an opinion?

- F "When baleen whales take a huge mouthful of seawater, they trap tiny animals and plants that drift in the sea."
- G "Whales, along with dolphins and porpoises, are members of a group of animals called cetaceans."
- H "Whales are interesting creatures because of the sounds they make."
- J "In addition, whales are sometimes accidentally caught in large fishing nets."

Tip: An opinion is something that someone believes. It is neither correct nor incorrect. Facts, on the other hand, can be proved. Read each statement and determine whether it can be proved or states how someone feels.

Go On

New York State English Language Arts Standards
13. (1) **Read for information and understanding.** Identify supporting details.
14. (1) **Read for information and understanding.** Compare and contrast information.
15. (1) **Read for information and understanding.** Identify supporting details.
16. (3) **Read for critical analysis and evaluation.** Distinguish between fact and opinion.

NYS Modeled Instruction: Reading 2

DIRECTIONS: In this section, you are going to read a story called "The Box in Lena's Cellar" and an article called "Uncovering the Past." You will answer questions and write about what you have read. You may look back at the story and the article as often as you like.

The Box in Lena's Cellar

Two weeks after the beginning of the school year, Lena's teacher announced that a crafts fair would be held at the end of September to display the rich culture of different families in the community. During the next several days, the students in Lena's class interviewed family members and neighbors to locate objects to exhibit at the crafts fair. Each student was expected to give a brief history of the object. Lena's friend Maria brought to class a rebozo her grandmother in Mexico had given her. It was a beautiful, long scarf that Maria modeled by wrapping it around her head and shoulders. Lena's friend Derek brought in turquoise and silver ornaments that his family had collected during their trip to Albuquerque.

Lena was stumped. She couldn't think of anything she might contribute. Her mother had a green thumb, and her father liked to tinker with automobiles, but no one had made a pot, created a quilt, or even built a doghouse.

One afternoon, as Lena was rummaging through a trunk in the cellar, she found a box of curious objects carved from some kind of stone. Each object seemed as heavy as a brick, but each shape was as fluid and elegant as flowing water. She took the box to her mother, who explained that it had belonged to an Inuit relative from the Canadian Arctic. Her mother was unable to tell her any more than this, however.

intrigued = interested

Intrigued by her discovery, Lena decided to investigate the objects by searching the Internet. After a little research, she found a Web site that discussed Inuit carvings. She began to look carefully at the objects in the box and realized that some were animals. One was the figure of a falcon in flight. Another was a whale. A third was a polar bear with a family of cubs. In the bottom of the box was the dark, heavy figure of a medicine man, a person who was believed to have healing powers. Lena learned that the sculptures were carved from soapstone, which is similar to marble.

When Lena brought the sculptures to class and delivered her report, Lena's teacher praised her imaginative research. The students crowded around Lena, asking if they might hold the objects. Maria and Derek said that they wanted to learn more about the Canadian Arctic and its culture.

17 How do you know that Lena's teacher and classmates are interested in the soapstone sculptures? Use details from the story to support your answer.

_____
_____
_____
_____
_____
_____
_____

> **Tip:** Usually you can figure out how people feel about something based on their actions in the story. Think about how Lena's class and her teacher react when she tells them about the sculptures.

Go On

New York State English Language Arts Standards
17. (2) **Read and write for literary response and expression.** Interpret plot.

18 What problem does Lena have at the beginning of the story, and how is it resolved? Use details from the story to support your answer.

_____

_____

_____

_____

_____

_____

_____

> **Tip:** Stories usually contain a problem and a solution. Reread the first two or three paragraphs to find what challenge Lena faces. Then read the rest of the story to see how she overcomes this problem.

New York State English Language Arts Standards
18. (2) **Read and write for literary response and expression.** Interpret plot.

Uncovering the Past

Scientists called archaeologists study human life in the past by looking at clues left by ancient peoples. Many of these clues, such as ancient tools and other man-made objects, are called artifacts. Artifacts are often buried underground, so archaeologists excavate, or uncover, buried artifacts through a process called an archaeological dig.

Archaeologists begin hunting for buried treasures by reading our oldest written records, such as ancient poetry, the Bible, or other historical records. For example, a man named Heinrich Schliemann (1822–1890) was fascinated by Homer's account of the Trojan War. Homer was a Greek poet who lived more than 3,000 years ago. Clues in the poem led Schliemann to the ancient site of Troy, in Turkey. After digging there, he found a Trojan fort, proving that Homer's poem the *Iliad* was based on a real war.

Before starting a "dig," archaeologists first study an area and form a plan. Then they dig into the earth and decide how big an excavation site to make. Sometimes digging machines safely remove the topsoil, but most work is done by hand with shovels and other small tools. As each object is discovered, archaeologists make an exact record of where it was found. They also make scale drawings and contour maps of the site to show how deep each object was buried. The artifacts are then cleaned and studied.

Archaeologists try to figure out the ages of artifacts by cross-dating, or comparing artifacts from one culture with those from another. In another technique, radio-carbon dating, scientists measure the radioactive carbon content of material that was once alive. This method can show the ages of artifacts made within the past 50,000 years. As new dating techniques are discovered, archaeologists will be able to tell even more about the past. Learning about the past can be hard work, but it is always very interesting.

Go On

19 What are the steps in an archaeological dig? Use information from the article in your answer.

_____
_____
_____
_____
_____
_____
_____

> **Tip:** Sometimes the steps in a process are presented in order. Often an author will include clue words, such as *first*, *next*, *then*, and *finally*, to indicate these steps. Review this article to find the steps in the process of an archaeological dig.

New York State English Language Arts Standards
19. (1) **Read and write for information and understanding.** Recognize and use organizational features.

NYS Modeled Instruction: Writing

20 Why is it important to learn about the past? Use information from BOTH "The Box in Lena's Cellar" and "Uncovering the Past" to support your answer.

In your answer, be sure to include:
- examples of what we can learn from studying the past
- details from BOTH the story and the article

You may PLAN your writing for Number 20 here if you wish, but do NOT write your final answer on this page. Your writing on this Planning Page will NOT count toward your final score. Write your final answer on a separate sheet of paper.

 Check your writing for correct spelling, grammar, and punctuation.

Tip: Organize your thoughts or make notes before you begin writing. Skim the story and the article, and write down words, phrases, and sentences that show why learning about the past is important.

Go On

New York State English Language Arts Standards
20. (3) Read and write for critical analysis and evaluation. Use critical analysis to evaluate ideas.

NYS Modeled Instruction: Listening

DIRECTIONS: In this section, you will listen to the story "History Lesson". Then you will answer some questions to show how well you understood what was read.

You will listen to the story twice. As you listen carefully, you may take notes on the articles anytime you wish during the readings. You may use these notes to answer the questions that follow. Use the space below for your notes.

Here are some words and definitions you will need to know before you listen to the story.
- **replica:** model
- **dogfights:** a type of combat involving fighter planes
- **tactics:** skills

> **Tip:** Listen carefully for details about the major characters and events of the story. In your notes, answer the questions *who, what, when, where, why,* and *how*. Write words and ideas instead of complete sentences.

Notes

21 At the beginning of the story, why is the narrator upset? Use details from the story to explain your answer.

_____

_____

_____

_____

_____

_____

_____

> **Tip:** Look at your listening notes to find out important details. Think about what the person telling the story, the narrator, says and does at the beginning of the story. This will show why the narrator feels upset.

Go On

New York State English Language Arts Standards
21. (2) **Listen and write for literary response and expression.** Describe characters and their motivations.

22 How does the narrator feel about his grandfather's World War I stories? Support your answer with details from the story.

_____
_____
_____
_____
_____
_____
_____

> **Tip:** A character's actions can help you understand how the character probably feels. Review your notes for information about how the narrator reacts when his grandfather tells him the stories.

STOP

New York State English Language Arts Standards
22. (2) **Listen and write for literary response and expression.** Make inferences about story events or characters.

NYS Modeled Instruction: Writing

23 In "History Lesson," the narrator's trip to his grandfather's house ends up being much different than he expected. Write about why you think "History Lesson" is a good title for this story. What lesson(s) does the narrator learn? Why is it the "best history lesson"?
- about World War I
- about his grandfather's interests

You may PLAN your writing for Number 23 here if you wish, but do NOT write your final answer on this page. Your writing on this Planning Page will NOT count toward your final score. Write your final answer on a separate sheet of paper.

 Check your writing for correct spelling, grammar, and punctuation.

Tip: Before writing, skim the story for important ideas about the narrator's "history lesson." When you write, be sure to answer each part of the question using details from the text.

STOP

New York State English Language Arts Standards
23. (3) **Write for critical analysis and evaluation.** Use critical analysis to evaluate ideas.

NYS Testing Program Test-Taking Tips

Now you are ready to try the Practice Test for the New York State English Language Arts Test. Use what you learned in the first section of this book to help you do well on the test. If you become familiar with the way the real test looks and the kinds of questions you will answer, you will be better prepared and more relaxed when you take the real test.

Remember these hints when you are taking the test.

- Listen carefully to the directions. Be sure to read all of the directions in the Practice Test section. Ask your teacher to explain any directions you do not understand.

- Read each selection carefully. Then read each question carefully. As you answer the questions, you may look back at the reading selections as often as you like.

- Listen carefully when a selection is read to you. Try to imagine the setting, characters, and action of the story as you listen. Take notes that will help you answer the questions after you have heard the story. Look back at your notes as often as you like when you answer questions about the story.

- Plan your time. You may want to glance quickly through the entire session before you begin answering questions in order to make the best use of the time you have.

- When you take the Practice Test, you will answer multiple-choice questions on a separate Answer Sheet. Fill in the answer bubbles completely. If you change your answer, be sure to erase your first answer completely.

- When you answer the open-ended questions, be sure to include details from the reading or listening selections to support your answers. You will write your answers in this book in the spaces provided.

- When you see this symbol, be sure to check your writing for correct spelling, grammar, capitalization, and punctuation.

To get the highest score on the open-ended questions, remember to

✓ organize and express your ideas clearly

✓ answer the question completely

✓ support your ideas with examples

Grade 6

New York State Testing Program

English Language Arts Practice Test

Book 1

Name _____

Reading

Session 1

Directions

The following story describes a young girl's voyage from Ireland to America. Read "Sailing to America." Then do Numbers 1 through 6.

Sailing to America

Eileen squeezed Padric's hand while baby Kate clung to Mama. Liam and Margaret stood with Papa, trying to look grown up and brave. My name is Mary. I am twelve years old and my family just arrived in America!

We'd been hoping to leave Ireland ever since 1845, when the potato crop was wiped out. Everyone in the country was starving. We saved money for over two years and hoped none of us would get sick. Mama danced a jig the night Papa said we could finally afford to go to America. We sailed to the Waterloo dock in Liverpool, England, the next day. None of us were sad to leave our damp little house, but I cried when I said goodbye to my friends.

Go On

We barely had enough money to be passengers on the *Globe*. We had only two trunks for all of our things. Mama took her sewing and cooking supplies. Papa packed his favorite tools. We also brought a few blankets, eating utensils, some extra shirts, and two sacks of flour. And I made sure to bring my rag doll Meg.

When the *Globe* started to set sail, the deck looked like a big party! People tossed hats and shouted goodbye to their friends and families on the dock. Some passengers played flutes, pipes, and violins. People young and old danced wherever they found room. Padric said he didn't care if he never saw Ireland again. I'm not sure I agree, but at least the most important parts of Ireland are still with me

Our sleeping quarters were very dark. We had two sets of cramped bunk beds for the eight of us. We could hear the hundreds of men, women, and children around us. We could smell them, too! This whole place was dirty and full of bad smells.

The trip was smooth sailing at first. But when the winds came, the ship tossed wildly, and I flew off my bunk. Boxes and barrels tumbled everywhere. Women grabbed onto their screaming children. It felt like the daunting winds would never stop blowing. Many people got sick or died during the storms. To make myself feel better, I whispered to Meg about all the things we'd do in America.

daunting = scary

Today, we finally ended our long six-week journey on the *Globe*. This morning, Padric dragged me out of my bed with the big news. He shouted for me to hurry as I grabbed Meg.

Everyone is now up on deck, pointing and waving. People are in a jubilant mood. Music has started and the *Globe* is like a party again. I can see New York City clear as day. After a long, hard journey, we finally made it!

1 The author probably wrote this story to

A convince readers to travel
B provide safety tips for boat passengers
C give information about the history of Ireland
D tell a story about a family of immigrants

2 When Mary says "the most important parts of Ireland are still with me," she is probably referring to

F the potato crop
G her family
H her friends
J her rag doll

3 Which of the following does Mary's family not bring on the trip?

A violins
B blankets
C sacks of flour
D sewing supplies

Go On

4 The conditions in the sleeping quarters can best be described as

F dusty
G healthy
H welcoming
J unpleasant

5 Mary and her family left Ireland because

A their house was too damp
B there were too many storms
C the potato crop was wiped out
D they did not have enough money to stay

6 Read these sentences from the story:

People are in a jubilant mood. Music has started and the Globe *is like a party again.*

In the first sentence, the word *jubilant* means

F happy
G tired
H unusual
J determined

Directions

The following article tells about different kinds of airships. Read "Lighter Than Air." Then do Numbers 7 through 12.

Lighter Than Air

The first airship people usually remember is the *Graf Zeppelin*, which flew on regularly scheduled trips between 1928 and 1937. However, it was back in 1852 that Henri Giffard flew a steam-powered airship between Paris and Trappes. Another Frenchman, Pierre Jullien, built and successfully tested two clockwork-driven, gas-filled airships in the 1850s.

Lighter-than-air aircraft can sail in the air due to the buoyancy of a balloon. The balloon is filled with a gas. The gas can be hot air, hydrogen, or helium. Hot-air balloons were among the earliest lighter-than-air aircraft. These balloons are open at one end. A burner close to the opening heats the air inside the balloon. Since hot air rises, the balloon rises up. A basket, called a gondola, holds the balloonist. Years ago, the gondola was made of lightweight wicker, but today synthetic materials are used. In time, people used buoyant gases other than hot air to fill these free-floating balloons.

buoyancy = ability to float

synthetic = man-made

Go On

A much more sophisticated lighter-than-air aircraft is the airship, also called a dirigible. *Dirigible* comes from a Latin word meaning "to direct." Dirigibles are powered by an engine and steered by a rudder.

This is a big advantage over a balloon, which cannot be steered. Balloonists have to rely on air currents to take them where they want to go. The passengers and crew of a dirigible ride in an enclosed gondola suspended from an enormous sealed balloon. The gas used in most modern dirigibles is helium.

Certainly the most famous airship in history was the *Hindenburg*. Like the ocean liner *Titanic*, the *Hindenburg* was truly elegant. Passengers traveled in luxury, dining at linen-covered tables beside huge picture windows. What a view they must have had! But on May 6, 1937, disaster struck. The *Hindenburg* had just crossed the Atlantic and had reached its final destination in Lakehurst, New Jersey. The ground crew was pulling the ship to the ground when it burst into flames. Thirty-five people were killed, most of them from jumping or falling from the burning vessel.

Tragically, the *Hindenburg* had a fatal flaw, but for a long time no one knew what it was. Some people thought the *Hindenburg* had been struck by lighting. Others suspected foul play. Many people blamed the tragedy on the fuel used to power the airship. Instead of helium, the ship's balloon was filled with hydrogen. But later, it appeared that hydrogen was not to blame for the disaster. It was the substance used to coat the outer fabric of the airship. The combination of dark iron oxide and aluminum paint is extremely flammable, and the pilot of the airship chose to land in an electrical storm. Electricity from the clouds ignited the airship. In seconds the entire tail burst into flames. The *Hindenburg* disaster ended the glory days of airships. Hot air balloon travel continues today, but it was a long time before people returned to the skies in strange ships that were lighter than air.

The Graf Zeppelin

7 The author probably wrote this passage to

  A inform readers about the history of airships
  B show the contribution the French made to air travel
  C entertain readers with stories of the *Titanic* and the *Hindenburg*
  D express disappointment that the dirigible is no longer in use

8 From the information in this article, what can the reader conclude about the end of the glory years of airships?

  F Dirigibles were uncomfortable to ride in.
  G People were afraid of dirigibles after the *Hindenburg* disaster.
  H Pilots found it difficult to steer dirigibles.
  J Dirigibles were dangerous because they used helium.

9 A dirigible is different from a free-floating balloon because

  A it contains a gondola
  B it uses a gas that is lighter than air
  C its pilots rely on air currents to take them where they want to go
  D it is powered by an engine and steered by a rudder

Go On

10 According to the article, a balloonist is

- **F** a person who collects models of balloons
- **G** a person who flies or rides in a balloon
- **H** a person who builds a balloon
- **J** a person who fills a balloon with hydrogen

11 What was the cause of the *Hindenburg* disaster?

- **A** foul play
- **B** hydrogen fuel
- **C** a lightning strike
- **D** flammable coating

12 Why can a hot-air balloon sail in the air?

- **F** It is powered by an engine.
- **G** It can be steered by a rudder.
- **H** Cold air causes the balloon to rise.
- **J** It is filled with a gas that is lighter than air.

Directions

The following story is about a young man who joins in on a family tradition. Read "The Soapstone Carver." Then do Numbers 13 through 20.

The Soapstone Carver

Aola watched his grandmother shape a piece of soapstone into a hunter, creating a tiny man holding a spear. That part of the sculpture would be delicate, so she worked slowly and deliberately. Aola wondered how his grandmother, small and hunched over, could carve for so many hours. He was a restless boy who enjoyed trapping and fishing with his father. But his father had just left their home in Arctic Bay, in Northern Canada, to seek a job elsewhere. He sent money to help out his family.

Like many of the Inuit people, Aola's family did not have much money. That is why his grandmother learned to carve soapstone in the 1960s, when outsiders became interested in the craft. Ever since Aola could remember, his grandmother had been producing these little figures—fish, bears, seal, people—designing whatever the traders considered "authentic." She worked until the skin on her hands peeled. When she became too uncomfortable, she stopped for a while to let her hands heal.

authentic = real

Today, Aola's grandmother seemed weary, and her expression was brooding and tense. She worked diligently, but her heart was not in it.

diligently = carefully

"Is something wrong? Have you had bad news?" He braced himself for what he would hear.

Grandmother frowned. "You should go and read your schoolbooks. It is almost time to make dinner." Winters were black and frigid. Aola would not feel free until the sun shone and the Inuit people followed their ancient custom of going to live on the land. In winter, families stayed in the village and made a living as best they could. The children were expected to study, much to Aola's annoyance.

"I want to know," Aola persisted. "I am nearly thirteen, no longer a child who has to have frightening things concealed from him."

"Your father has lost his job."

Aola understood the significance of her words. There would be less money for clothing, food, and other necessities. Grandmother would have to work much harder until his father could send money. She earned some income from her art, but she could not work as steadily as she had as a young woman. He stared at his grandmother's hands, which looked dry and sore. His own hands, callused from rough play, looked strong and firm. He had heard that Inuit art was valuable in other parts of the world, where it was displayed in galleries and bought by collectors. Aola took a deep breath.

Go On

"Grandmother, I am ready to learn to carve."

His grandmother looked up at him, unprepared for his comment. To his surprise, the elderly woman did not argue with him. Instead, she began talking to him in a way that was unfamiliar.

"When you hold a stone, you have to imagine that there is something inside, eager to come out. It is waiting for you to find it. This stone held a hunter, impatient to use his spear. I was tired when I thought about how much effort it would take to dig him out of this piece of stone, but I knew that he was there. So I carved and carved until I saw his shape. Then I had to work with all my skill and attention to make the details come out right."

Aola understood. "I want to carve," he reminded her. He did not even know if he meant what he said, but he wanted to earn money to help his family. "Do you have a stone for me?"

"You can start with this one," she replied, removing a rough stone from a basket. "What do you see in this piece?"

Aola carefully studied the flat, oval stone and envisioned water and movement.

"A kayak," he decided.

"Good," Grandmother smiled. She chose a tool from her box. Slowly and painstakingly she guided his hands over the stone until he felt the blade sink in, starting its long labor.

13 Which of these best expresses the theme of this story?

- A It is always best to let adults deal with their problems alone.
- B You are never too old to learn a new hobby.
- C Sometimes the young can step in to help solve the problems of adults.
- D It is important to always listen to the advice of grandparents.

14 Aola decides to learn soapstone carving because

- F he admires the beautiful artwork that his grandmother carves
- G his grandmother believes he has a special talent for the art
- H he hopes to impress his grandmother by becoming an artist
- J he knows his family needs more money because his father has lost his job

15 Which of the following from the story shows that Grandmother thinks Aola is ready to learn to carve?

- A "Today, Aola's grandmother seemed weary, and her expression was brooding and tense."
- B "Aola understood the significance of her words. There would be less money for clothing, food, and other necessities."
- C "His grandmother looked up at him, unprepared for his comment."
- D "To his surprise, the elderly woman did not argue with him. Instead, she began talking to him in a way that was unfamiliar."

16 Grandmother realizes that Aola is ready to learn the art of carving because

- F Aola is almost thirteen years old and seems mature for his age
- G Aola understands the shape and possibilities of his stone
- H Aola handles the carving tools well
- J Aola works until the skin on his hands peels

Go On

Session 1 NYS Testing Program Practice Test • 35

17 From the actions of Aola's father, the reader can conclude that he

    A loves to travel
    B cares about his family
    C hopes that Aola will mature
    D does not like Arctic Bay

18 This passage is an example of

    F historical fiction
    G an adventure
    H fantasy
    J a short story

19 Read this sentence from the story:

Winters were black and frigid.

In this sentence, the word *frigid* means

    A happy
    B cold
    C sunny
    D sad

20 According to the story, which of the following is an ancient custom of the Inuit people?

    F soap making
    G living on the land
    H trapping
    J spear fishing

Directions

The following article tells about the famous scientist Jane Goodall. Read "Jane and the Chimps." Then do Numbers 21 through 26.

Jane and the Chimps

You may have heard that chimpanzees are a lot like human beings, but a woman named Jane Goodall learned from experience just how much like humans they really are. Jane Goodall was 26 years old when she moved to Tanzania to study the chimpanzees in Gombe National Park. For Jane, it was the chance of a lifetime. She had dreamed of traveling to Africa and studying wildlife since she was a small child. When she moved to Gombe, she not only studied chimps but also lived with them in the wild and made them her friends.

Jane had no training in animal behavior when she first arrived in Gombe, but she had a desire to learn. She had a curiosity about chimps, and she longed to learn how they lived in the wild. She also had no problem living in the wild herself. Jane lived in the forest in conditions that most people could not tolerate. She lived among snakes and insects and aggressive baboons. Some of the insects carried diseases such as malaria. Jane did not let any of these threats stop her from doing her work.

> aggressive = tending to attack

Jane Goodall's experience in Gombe began shortly after she met a scientist named Louis Leakey. Jane first worked as Dr. Leakey's assistant. Then he sent her to Africa to observe a community of chimps who lived in the forest. At first the chimps were afraid of Jane, so she kept her distance until they learned to trust her. Finally, they allowed her to move into the forest and become their friend.

Go On

Jane was able to make friends with the chimps because she respected them. She could see that they would not harm her, and they understood that she would not harm them. Learning to communicate with the chimps, Jane discovered that each of them had a distinct personality. Jane marveled as the chimps expressed fear and joy, as they hunted with tools they made, and as they tended their babies with loving care. Many mornings Jane got up early to observe the chimps throughout the day. Each day in the forest brought new surprises from these creatures.

Jane Goodall surprised the world by living alone with wild animals, but she surprised the world even more when she learned that chimpanzees have thoughts and feelings much like human beings. She learned that they can form relationships, and she came to know each of the chimps in the community in Gombe as an individual. Anyone who has a chance to read about Jane or listen to her speak will learn how strongly she feels about allowing chimpanzees to remain in the forests. Many people who study chimps keep them in contained areas—such as zoos—where they behave much differently than they do in the wild. Jane learned all of these amazing things by living with these chimpanzees in their natural setting.

Jane continued her work with the chimps after she left Gombe. In 1977, she founded the Jane Goodall Institute. Jane's goal was to support research on chimps in the wild and to discourage people from removing chimps from their natural surroundings. Jane's love for all animals is the reason she could live with the chimps and gain their trust. She made the study of chimps her life work. She also made it a goal to educate people on the importance of keeping her friends, the chimpanzees, in the forests. She saw for herself that that's where they truly belong.

21 Jane observed the chimps from far away because

   A they did not like her
   B she did not want to frighten them
   C it was unsafe to go into the forest
   D she was afraid they would hurt her

22 The main purpose of Jane's work was to

   F make animals her friends
   G teach chimps how to communicate
   H live alone in the wild
   J observe chimps in their natural setting

23 The author would probably agree that chimpanzees

   A need to be treated like humans
   B can never be fully trusted
   C deserve to be treated respectfully
   D want to have friendships with people

Go On

24 The author probably mentions Dr. Leakey to

F explain why Jane went to work in Gombe
G explain that Jane did not work alone
H tell about Dr. Leakey's work with the chimps
J tell why Dr. Leakey was an important person

25 Which of the following did Jane <u>not</u> observe chimps doing in Gombe National Park?

A hunting with tools
B forming relationships
C expressing fear and joy
D living in contained areas

26 This article is organized using mostly

F time order
G compare and contrast
H cause and effect
J order of importance

STOP

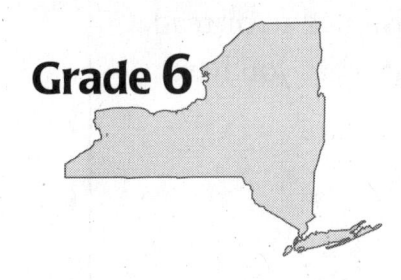

New York State Testing Program

Grade 6

English Language Arts Practice Test

Book 2

Name _____

This test will ask you to write about selections you have listened to or read. Your writing will NOT be scored on what you think about what you have read or heard. It WILL be scored on

- clear organization and expression of ideas
- accurate and complete answers
- examples that support your ideas
- interesting and enjoyable writing
- correct use of grammar, spelling, punctuation, and paragraphs

This symbol will remind you to plan and check your writing.

Session 2

Part 1: Listening

Directions

In this part of the test, you will listen to the story "Hector's Choice." Then you will answer some questions to show how well you understood what was read.

You will listen to the story twice. As you listen carefully, you may take notes on the story anytime you wish during the readings. You may use these notes to answer the questions that follow. Use the space on page 44 for your notes.

Here is a term and definition you will need to know before you listen to the story:

- **gear ratio:** a relationship between the number of teeth on meshing gears that affects performance

Go On

Notes

27 This story is titled "Hector's Choice." What is Hector's choice in the story? Use details from the story in your answer.

_____

_____

_____

_____

_____

_____

_____

28 Why is Hector worried about Rachel? Use details from the story to support your answer.

29 At the beginning of the story, how do you know that Hector really wants a bicycle? Use details from the story in your answer.

_____

_____

_____

_____

_____

_____

_____

STOP

Session 2

Part 2: Writing

Directions

Planning Page

You may PLAN your writing for Number 30 here if you wish, but do NOT write your final answer on this page. Your writing on this Planning Page will NOT count toward your final score. Write your final answer on Pages 49 and 50.

Answer →

30. In "Hector's Choice," Hector does something nice for his sister by buying her a puppy. Do you think that Hector made the right decision? What do you learn about Hector from the choice he made? Use details from the story to support your answer.

In your story, be sure to include:
- whether you think Hector made the right decision
- why you feel the choice was good or bad
- what you learned about Hector based on his choice

✓ Check your writing for correct spelling, grammar, capitalization, and punctuation.

Go On

Session 3

Part 1: Reading

Directions

In this part of the test, you are going to read an article called "Morning Star, Evening Star" and a poem called "Harvest Moon." You will answer questions and write about what you have read. You may look back at the story and poem as often as you like.

Go On

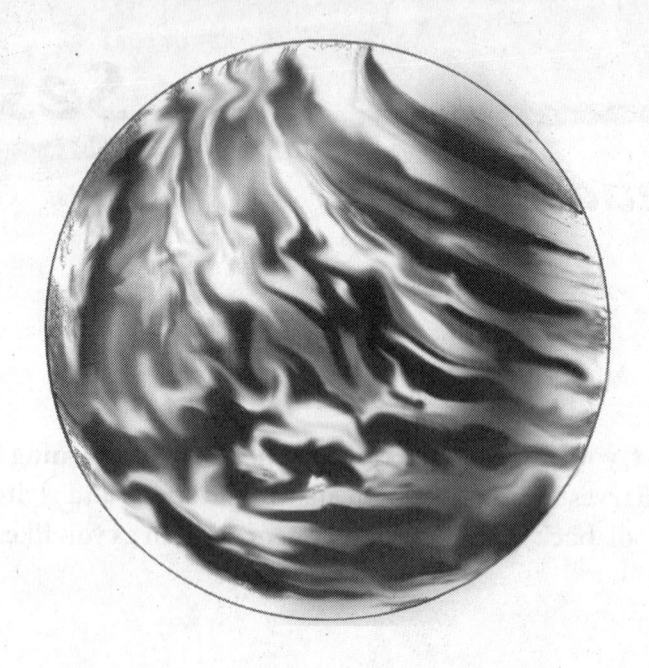

Morning Star, Evening Star

Planets confused people for a long time. Planets looked like stars, but they did not act like stars. They wandered back and forth across the sky, and they appeared in a different place every night. People who watched the sky long ago did not know that stars and planets were different objects. Except for the moon, every light in the night sky looked like a small, bright dot. Some of those dots shone brighter than others, however, and one of those dots shone brightest of all.

We know today that the brightest dot that lights the night is Venus. Venus is a planet, but it was the most popular "star" in the ancient world. Sometimes this "star" rose in the morning ahead of the sun and lit the eastern sky. Other times it lit the western sky at night and it stayed above the horizon long after the sun disappeared.

Venus mystified ancient skywatchers. They labeled Venus "Morning Star" when they saw it shining brightly at dawn, and they labeled it "Evening Star" when they saw it shining brightly after sunset. People who watched Venus spent a lot of time creating fun and exciting legends about it. These legends tried to explain why a "star" appeared to rule both the morning and the night. Many of these legends featured Morning Star and Evening Star as different objects, objects that looked like stars but that acted strangely. Still, even though ancient people didn't quite understand these two bright lights in the sky, they were comforted by them. Many believed that Morning Star and Evening Star were watching over people to keep them safe.

Today we know that stars are much different from planets. Stars shine by themselves, for one thing. They are simply burning balls of gas. Planets, on the other hand, get their light from the sun. Some planets are made of gas, but Mercury, Venus, and Mars are made largely of rock and metal. This makes their structure similar to Earth, not stars. Of all planets, Venus is most similar to Earth. It shines so brightly because it is the closest planet to Earth and because it is surrounded by clouds that reflect the sun's light.

People long ago could see that planets moved, but they did not understand how they moved until instruments called telescopes were invented and scientists could see the movements up close. Scientists learned that planets orbit the sun and that each planet moves in its own orbit and at its own speed. The orbit of Venus is closer to the sun than the orbit of Earth. This explains a lot about its curious behavior. Venus always moves in and out of the sun's light as it moves around the sky.

31 What are some ways that planets and stars are different? Use information from the article to support your answer.

32 Why was the planet Venus so confusing to ancient skywatchers? Use information from the article to explain your answer.

Harvest Moon

Drowsy after a day of carnival fun,

Rocked gently homeward in the car,

I have almost fallen asleep

when the moon rises like a dream

outside my back-seat window.

It is the world's largest Ferris wheel,

bright as a beacon,

welcoming all riders.

It is a giant pumpkin slowly ripening,

outgrowing its protective ground cover.

It is the face of a smiling friend

who wants to play hide-and-seek

behind the highway's bare trees.

I smile back at my friend

and drift off to sleep.

Maybe I'll play when I awaken.

33 How does the author use metaphors in this poem? Use details from the poem to support your answer.

_____

_____

_____

_____

_____

_____

_____

Session 3

Part 2: Writing

Directions

Planning Page

You may PLAN your writing for Number 34 here if you wish, but do NOT write your final answer on this page. Your writing on this Planning Page will NOT count toward your final score. Write your final answer on Pages 59 and 60.

Answer ➡

34 Both "Morning Star, Evening Star" and "Harvest Moon" tell about skywatchers. Why do people enjoy watching the sky? Is skywatching a good way of learning about the world? Use information from BOTH the article and the poem to support your answer.

In your answer, be sure to include:
- examples of why people like to watch the sky
- examples of how skywatching does, or does not, teach us about the world
- details from BOTH the poem and the article

✓ Check your writing for correct spelling, grammar, and punctuation.

Go On

NYS Testing Program Answer Sheet

STUDENT'S NAME — LAST, FIRST, MI

SCHOOL:
TEACHER:
FEMALE ○   MALE ○

BIRTH DATE — MONTH / DAY / YEAR

Jan, Feb, Mar, Apr, May, Jun, Jul, Aug, Sep, Oct, Nov, Dec

GRADE ③ ④ ⑤ ⑥ ⑦ ⑧

Achieve New York State English Language Arts Grade 6

The New York State assessments in English Language Arts are published by CTB/McGraw-Hill. Such company has neither endorsed nor authorized this test-preparation book.

TEST
Book 1, Session 1

1. Ⓐ Ⓑ Ⓒ Ⓓ
2. Ⓕ Ⓖ Ⓗ Ⓙ
3. Ⓐ Ⓑ Ⓒ Ⓓ
4. Ⓕ Ⓖ Ⓗ Ⓙ
5. Ⓐ Ⓑ Ⓒ Ⓓ
6. Ⓕ Ⓖ Ⓗ Ⓙ
7. Ⓐ Ⓑ Ⓒ Ⓓ
8. Ⓕ Ⓖ Ⓗ Ⓙ
9. Ⓐ Ⓑ Ⓒ Ⓓ
10. Ⓕ Ⓖ Ⓗ Ⓙ
11. Ⓐ Ⓑ Ⓒ Ⓓ
12. Ⓕ Ⓖ Ⓗ Ⓙ
13. Ⓐ Ⓑ Ⓒ Ⓓ
14. Ⓕ Ⓖ Ⓗ Ⓙ
15. Ⓐ Ⓑ Ⓒ Ⓓ
16. Ⓕ Ⓖ Ⓗ Ⓙ
17. Ⓐ Ⓑ Ⓒ Ⓓ
18. Ⓕ Ⓖ Ⓗ Ⓙ
19. Ⓐ Ⓑ Ⓒ Ⓓ
20. Ⓕ Ⓖ Ⓗ Ⓙ
21. Ⓐ Ⓑ Ⓒ Ⓓ
22. Ⓕ Ⓖ Ⓗ Ⓙ
23. Ⓐ Ⓑ Ⓒ Ⓓ
24. Ⓕ Ⓖ Ⓗ Ⓙ
25. Ⓐ Ⓑ Ⓒ Ⓓ
26. Ⓕ Ⓖ Ⓗ Ⓙ

Book 2, Sessions 2 and 3
Answer open-ended questions directly in the book.